the flap pamphlet series

Prickle

open, read, turn

Prickle

the flap pamphlet series (No. 33)
Printed and Bound in the United Kingdom

Published by the flap series, 2024
the pamphlet series of flipped eye publishing
All Rights Reserved

Cover Design by Petraski
Series Design © flipped eye publishing, 2010

Author Photo © Lola Webster
First Edition
Copyright © **Rachel Cleverly**, 2024

ISBN-13: 978-1-905233-86-1

Prickle

Rachel Cleverly

For Mum, Dad, Luke and Nat

Contents | *Prickle*

Toil 9
Off the Clock 10
Streaming 12
[Enter me] 13
We Have Gathered in Lieu of Something 14
Flesh Prison 17
Things Which Make My Life Difficult and My Writing Bad 18
Submissions 19
Baby on Board 20
Love Bugs 21
Back to Work 24
Best Seat in the House 25
Is Harry Kane Real or Is He FIFA? 26
Two girls 27
In Lidl 28
No Good News Today 30
Spread 31
The Year Prickled 32
Acknowledgements 33

Toil

My employers force me to take holiday.

I don't have the money to go anywhere.

I spend the morning watching pigeons

eating vomit in the Asda car park.

I'd rather be at work, with my camera off.

I don't like to be involved. I find

a listing for free comedy. I am hot

in the audience, in the dark, my beer green

in the stage light. A comedian impersonates

a paper straw. She says: *Don't pretend*

you've not been watching me. Buy me a drink.

I sip my beer and feel anaemic and the comedian

inhales a glass of clear liquid. The set ends

when my tongue is coated with something

the texture of algae. I am wilting in the dark.

I hold the glass between my legs and clap.

Off the Clock

I'd described the flat as *affordably small*.

There was only one viewing. When we reached the end,
I left him a moment to imagine living between the walls.
I could hear the opening of drawers from
the kitchen/living area. I worried he'd discover
how few creams I owned, how little I had spent
on taking care. I couldn't afford to be alone.

The viewer, a senior consultant, moved in.

The senior consultant was an expert
in monetisation and growth. He'd gotten too old
to stay in Hackney, in the warehouse
he'd rented with sixteen emerging artists,
more than one of them identifying as
a professional clown.

The senior consultant offered me advice freely.

He taught me to turn the heating on when I was home alone.
He taught me to stack the dishwasher, cutlery sharp side up
for a thorough clean. He taught me not to fear
use-by dates, unwashed fruit, the TV Licence people.
That's bad for you, he'd say, walking in on me in the dark,
aiming boiling water at an unseeable mug.

The senior consultant ran 60 kilometres a week.

I wished he'd ask me to come running with him
until he'd asked me to come running with him.
He professionally advised I start out on my own.
I was unattractively self-conscious of my stride.

He could do a half in sub-90 if he tried. He liked to devote
his time to recognising the scarcity of obstacles in his life.

Try it, he'd said, professionally.

I tried. By lap two of the park I'd recognised
I had three healthy father figures
and no imminent risk of unemployment.
Lap three, the sun was setting:
I couldn't breathe. At the canal a man
pulled his penis out at me.

The senior consultant was waiting in the kitchen/living area.

He charged by the hour and with all my fretting
felt that he was never off the clock. He'd heard me, at night,
walking into and out of rooms, forgetting things, going back.
He could not understand how I did things without
interrogating why I should, until he'd asked me to stop.
I had wasted years pairing socks at inconvenient times.

The senior consultant could afford to be alone.

I sent him pictures of each thing I fixed:
the broken blinds, the radiator. I cleaned
that bit between the floorboards. He was
encouraging but preferred not sharing a bathroom.
I look around my flat and see what there is to do.
How I lived before. The cutlery. The fruit. My god.

Streaming

I've been a lot more leaky lately. I can't stop
crying. There's normally something
else to blame it on – fungus allergies, which I don't have,
or loneliness,   which I often do.

My biggest thrill is hiding
from everyone I love
and picking off eczema scabs
                where no one can tell me to stop.

Jay and I still haven't
touched. He tried to kiss me at the Tate Modern
a week after that boy had fallen
from the roof to his death. Can a person really be

                dry-eyed?
Not completely, like an egg
before the mayonnaise.
Like a hardboiled egg   but furry.

I manage to limit the scratching
to Jay's trips to the bathroom.
We are in a vegetarian all-you-can-eat. I ask Jay
to describe me in five words. He thinks

for a moment. I match him on the pace of his eating,
cucumber slice for cucumber slice, meatball for meatball.
Jay mumbles *dry* three times,
    and   can't think of two more words.

[Enter me]

The sound of typing and checking the weather. Looking out. Refreshing the weather again. // I called the AI by the wrong name and blushed. // This is what you'd predicted. The answers we'd looked for in each other grew into something Googleable. The sound of typing. The slugs were out. // I felt sick. // Sit upright for months being unsuccessful at various things, adequate at few. Attend self-inflicted interviews. Fail acts of preparation. Look at notes. Disguise that you are reading off of your notes. Lose place. // I was reading off of my notes. // It had been raining. Lost links were requested in broken language: *Can you send the guy eating italian food wrong tiktok?* There was no need to finish a thought. // In my next iteration my hands will learn to sleep. //

We Have Gathered in Lieu of Something

I invite Katy to an award ceremony
for a literary prize. Everyone in the room
is looking for the winner, who looks
like everyone in the room.

> *It's great for recognition, congratulations.*
> *Where are your kids tonight?*
> *How far are you*
> *from your poems?*

I perform myself then introduce Katy
to the writers in the room: *This is Katy, she works in paediatrics
and doesn't read poetry.*
She works in a psychiatric unit, puts salt in her porridge.

I have found myself beside a table the height of my elbow
so I lean on it. I am offered a variety of free things
which I accept, then feel bad about. A man in the corner is
shouting *Everything is your fault!* at his daughter.

Katy promises to buy everyone's book. She makes a list
of half-heard titles, pressing them into her phone,
adding the poet who spells out her surname whilst explaining
the symptoms of delayed onset PTSD.

We are not leaving fast enough. No one knows
who owns which free tote. A waiter
tells me he is an actor,
handing me someone else's coat.

Some of the poets are also actors.
Some of the poets are also waiters.

Some of the actors are also poets.
One of these people is Katy, on her phone.

Someone says,
                          Pub?
I am researching my journey home
but being the first to leave

seems like the last thing my character would do.
I am swapping phones to make sure
this never ends. Katy is talking
to a teacher about working with kids

and reductions in government funding.
I congratulate the teacher for being on the shortlist
          (*I'd never heard donkeys versified with such zest*)
but he isn't, I've got the wrong person, everyone looks

like everyone else. We all look like winners here.
I am performing myself again.
          We all work with young people!
How bad can someone who works with children be?

I imagine my shame
is the olive
I am stabbing
with a wooden pick.

I could say *I only work with young people*
in an administrative capacity,
instead I repeat
          Katy doesn't read poetry!

Katy tells me I am behaving quite unlike myself
which is actually exactly something
someone like me would do.
          Another olive? Ok!

The teacher has walked away at this point,
someone has mistakenly bought him
a drink to congratulate him
on the award he didn't win.

If I was bought a drink for every award I hadn't won
I'd have an empty glass to put each of my olive pips in.
Katy's face says she's ready to go.
We wave to people who wouldn't

have waved at us, such as the teacher
who now thinks I am Katy and work
in paediatric mental health
and don't read poetry.

I'd like to say the only time
I've restrained a child is metaphorically
but look at poor Katy,
dragged out on a Wednesday.

Has the writer who read
the poem about the donkey
left? I'd really love
to congratulate him.

Flesh Prison

There was a doll's house in my parents' living room.
We found it on the road in St Albans. I hadn't asked.
Mum wanted it. She already has a real house.

Grandad lives in a retirement home near my parents.
You've got to come and sort it out, he says to Dad. He thinks
the nurses are trying to artificially inseminate him. *Okay,*

says Dad, *and what did they give you for lunch?*
My parents have been considering moving to a place
they don't want to live to be closer to me,

or my siblings, or both. We will reduce the time we spend
squinting at photos of broken appliances. We might watch
each other malfunction in life-size. They will have to wait

until Grandad dies. That won't be long,
or so they've been telling us for fifteen years.
He's closer than ever.

Things Which Make My Life Difficult and My Writing Bad

Less time working
more time fucking up my back

1000+ unread messages   I know
this morning I woke up to (1) new email

beee-dhunk   my inbox
has never felt so purposeless

since they've been archived   collapsed into a folded
thing which threatens to be full   as a tummy

all my family are on calls to each other
in different rooms with unprofessional backgrounds

I've turned an ironing board into a standing desk
I cc'd myself into a nap with you even in sleep I enter formally

none of my habits seem bad now I have someone else
to check my spam

did you notice my hair has grown
when you get this can you shake my hand

Submissions

All my hurt recounted
anecdotally. Like putting something
in the wrong place consistently.
Reading 18,000 poems is enough
to make you want to write a good one
or none at all. I tell the story of
my weekend to each colleague
as they enter the office.

In my anecdote
I am at a party. I lie
about how I feel
about the people I am with.
My anecdote has been typed up.
How disappointing. All
these shades of rehappening
which never happened, or not like that.

My anecdote would be impressive
if the administrator hadn't been watching
through each reimagining. He peers over
when I am writing poems but should be
checking emails. *The good ideas!*
They're leaving me! I shout. I feel composed
and uncomplicated, stripping
the skin from my thumb.

Baby on Board

Each time I see a badge
I look at the stomach
of the person wearing it.
Not that pregnant, I think.
I could surely be that pregnant
without knowing. If a gunman
boarded the bus and
picked off the passengers
one-by-one, it would be
frowned upon for me not to volunteer myself
first, perhaps using my body as a shield
to save the pregnant lady. My unknown
foetus and I would be the first to go.
I suppose I should get up
from my seat, and I do, glaring.

I want your seat not your life,
says the pregnant lady.

I am not an awful specimen. I am
trying to like children more,
especially those produced
by my friends inappropriately
at barbecues. I am teaching myself
not to imagine the noise
they would make if I dropped
the variously-sized offspring
on patio floors. Except the newborns.
Their heads. Their necks.

Love Bugs

Boyfriend and I have been arguing
since I've begun sleeping with
my phone torch on. I recently started
moving his things in;
he recently started trying to leave me.
That's when I spot a beetle-like body in the dark.
I ask Vicki, an exterminator, to connect on LinkedIn.
We DM a bit. I send tasteful nudes of my back
sloppily covered in bites. I discover these are
stains from my (homemade!) coffee facemask
which somehow seems less like self-care
and more disgusting now.

> The bugs are decidedly unattracted to me.
> I remain impressively bite-free
> making me actually feel pretty dirty,
> like even they don't want me.
> They love Boyfriend though.
> I'm worried he likes them too,
> so, I wet my sheets with eco-friendly bug repellent
> until he tries to excuse himself from staying at mine.

After the nudes, Vicki, the exterminator, leaves me on read,
then four hours later: *Try and get your landlord to buy a new bed.*

> *Honestly*, says estate agent to me,
> *communications with your guy are patchy*
> *– he works somewhere proper exotic*
> *like Congo, not a lot of service there.*

My landlord's LinkedIn lists him
as a retired antiques dealer in Benidorm.

> I, however, wear the coat of a nervous traveller
> after Vicki, my exterminator, told me
> the Northern Line carries three times more pests
> than the average Overground carriage.
> > *It does now!*
> I think as I come back from Boyfriend's:
> crawling past Kentish Town with a bag
> full of bed linen, I'm too scared to sit
> so I hover above the seat in a sort of squat.

Thankfully, I'm not allowed over after his mum saw me
pulling a shrunken hoodie from the dryer: I whispered
I'll be keeping this for your grandkids.

> Boyfriend starts to stay at mine to avoid
> an infestation at his own house.
> Our relationship problems have been exterminated
> since we're isolated in the flat. We steam our sheets
> together, each day, fifteen times
> though both bugs and him
> aren't really up for anything –
> he wraps his arms around a knee, rolls over,
> turns his back to me. It's threaded with love bites
> no bigger than the head of a needle.

So, I slipper-shuffle through the flat to pee
and slipper-shuffle back to find him
on his front, shirtless, legs trapped
in the flap of pyjama bottoms. He's hugging
a bug, and I'm jealous, itching
for the feel of tiny teeth on my shoulder.
A bug, I say, head roaring
over the tumble dryer's snore. Louder,
A bug, until he hears. We assess the bedroom guest
like a passionless middle-aged couple
inviting a third person under the sheets.
The bug looks relaxed: he's done this before.

      Boyfriend pinches him like a loose piece of string,
            rolls him between finger and thumb.
                    The bug stretches up a flirty arm.
                          He's waving, knows this is
                        the end.

He's saying, *Goodbye Vicki,*
goodbye co-habiting, and goodbye Boyfriend.
Boyfriend's hand flinches into a fist.
He unpicks each finger, loosening slowly
the stitches of my life in his palm.
A bloodstain dot sleeps on his pointer.
The size of a needle. Little prick.

Back to Work

This morning I made eye contact with myself
for the entirety of a 48-minute video interview.
My manager asked me where I see myself in five years' time.

>Mum says I am careless.
>I forget to switch off the hob,
>never have any hand cream,
>walk around with my phone on 6%,
>windows propped open when I'm out,
>Marmite sucking itself shut,
>the lid only part-way screwed.
>*What are you trying to do*, Mum says, *kill us?*

Best Seat in the House

If I had thought about it   I might have known
you would not look   out the window at me,
face inches from your own.   I followed a feeling,
had arrived keys in hand   and not gone in but stood
outside, watching you wash up   and waiting for you
to notice me.   I'd sat in your seat before I left,
pushed my back   up against the armrest and unspun.
The view from there   was clearer. I didn't have to turn
my neck   to look at the TV.
Everything in the room   could be seen
except those piles of things I was   hiding,
which were hidden.   No wonder
you had taken   that seat for yourself.
No wonder   you were unused to looking out the window.

Is Harry Kane Real or Is He FIFA?

Either way you're shouting. You tell me not to
shit on the importance of working-class culture.

I don't see the point in polo or golf
or healthy snacks or charging my phone

fully either. You're watching...
almost-goals. I could come

to feel at ease between barbecue crisps and
when you're not shouting.

I say, *If all my Sundays are this I might be ok.* You reply:
                                                Huh.

The men have their little pixel-faces screwed up
like something's gone wrong. I tell you I just said

something really nice.
You say, *Shut your face.*

It's not clear if you're talking to me
or the referee.

Two girls

I went to school with
spot me and I assert my success
by throwing myself into the road.
Only I exist in this city. They exist
at village fairs, in wellies with their dogs.

When I go back home
I see people that I know
looking older, much older.
How many children they have.
How little they pick at their hands.

I'll know I'm truly old
when they are all driving instructors.

I walk out in front of an L-plated car, stopped
just in time. The instructor leans across to wave
a fillet of hand. He nods.

Go ahead, says the
brake pedal,
go right ahead.

In Lidl

I almost want him
to see me. I am cactus-like
with items, not yet at
the point of rethinking
almost-purchases before putting
almost all of it back. Almost

everyone is in apathetic
disguise. I wasn't thinking
of him when I should or might
have been, given that almost
everyone looked like him.
I hadn't seen him since

our fourth date, but I had only
just thought I'd seen him
in the middle aisle, which almost
always holds things I haven't planned for,
but could do with. It hadn't been him,
actually, obviously, but almost.

I do think about him
often: e.g. when someone
I'm sleeping with hits me,
or each time I sit on a roof.
My boyfriend has recently
told me I often use e.g.

when I mean i.e. He explained
the distinction, and I'd thought
about him then, too.
When I see him, not almost, but

actually, he is in the queue,
almost at the front.

I am thinking of him and
looking at him, looking like almost
everybody else. I almost want him
to see me, too. He can't: I am too
many people away, holding onto fruit
I am almost ready to put back.

No Good News Today

I feel upset   at a child's birthday party
the single-use plastic   the apocalypse   boyfriend's brother
rents a bouncy castle blows it up   in the garden

a journalist I respected for a long time for defending
views which I believe in
but am unable to articulate
posts   *still looking for people with experiences*
                 of trying to break a generational curse
                 DMs open

when my nephew is nappyless and free
he shouts TOTALLY NAKED until slipped into something clean
TAKE IT OFF TAKE IT OFF TAKE IT OFF   he kicks

he is the future   let's hope
he remembers the ramifications of party poppers
                                        on the earth

boyfriend's dad is sorry I've lost my job so I remind him
                 not fired   *just not renewed*
       there's little else to offer   he asks
whether my last landlord has returned
       my deposit   *no she's stolen it*

Spread

The worst thing I have ever said in a fight is,
You don't even care about recycling! My hands are bleeding.
And my nipples, too. It is every bit like me to roll my eyes as everything
oozes apart. You say you want a future with me but if you get caught stealing
bags for life from Sainsbury's they'll never let us adopt. My niche allergies
are kissing my cheeks again, the redness has spread to the lip now. All my rashes joined up
to ruin me. You are unimpressed by my symptoms. There are steroids on my steroids.
I am punctured by sensitive creams. It's all infection here. I'm fitting my things into a tote
and carrying it through the carpark. The nicest thing you've said to me is,
If I was as scared of everything as you are then I'd be dead.

The Year Prickled

All of my friends were doing
at home laser hair removal
on their arse cracks. I was
hoping not to get myself
involved. The body
will sort itself out. I've lost
hours curating
an exhibition of myself.
Removing and re-adding
bread to my diet. I'm tired
of doing ridiculous things
with absolute devotion.
A whole face sheds
under my nail. I resolve
to throw less away.

Acknowledgements

Thank you to all of the staff at flipped eye, and especially my editor Jacob Sam-La Rose, for helping, advising and shaping.

Thank you to the following prizes and publications where some of this work was first shared: *And Other Poems, Channel, Ink Sweat & Tears,* The Manchester Cathedral Poetry Competition, *The North, Tentacular* and the Winchester Poetry Prize.

Thank you to the Barbican Young Poets 2021-22 and 2022-23 for company, understanding and feedback. Thank you to my brilliant Wriot collective, the first poets to make me feel part of the poetry community. Thank you to Apples and Snakes for funding an Arvon Foundation residential course where the idea for this pamphlet began to scratch at my brain.

Thank you to the following: Simon Keane, Gee Kirby, Jamie McGeown, Charlotte Moll, Micaela Pirani-Watson, Polina Pogudina, Fran Spree, Kez Swiecicki and Lola Webster.

Thank you to Julien for meeting my meanness with kindness, and to Mum, Dad, Luke and Natalie - I write about you so often because I love you so much.